LINES OFF

HUGO WILLIAMS

Lines Off

FABER & FABER

First published in 2019
by Faber & Faber Ltd
Bloomsbury House
74–77 Great Russell Street
London WC1B 3DA

Typeset by Hamish Ironside
Printed in the UK by TJ International Ltd, Padstow, Cornwall

A CIP record for this book is available from the British Library

ISBN 978-0-571-34975-3

2 4 6 8 10 9 7 5 3 1

To My Granddaughter Silver

You began with a dot,
ground into the paper, smashed,
hammered home.
You set out from there
with a look of defiance,
moving your hand up and down,
round and round,
in a series of spirals and swirls,
then suddenly stopped
and looked me in the eye.

The resulting description
of red in action,
with crumbs from a broken crayon,
inspired me to take up my pen
and make a new start.
I moved my hand up and down,
round and round,
in a series of scribbles and scrawls,
which turned out
something like this.

Acknowledgements

To the editors of *Literary Review*, *London Review of Books*, *New Statesman*, *Poetry Review*, *PN Review*, *The Spectator*, *Times Literary Supplement*, *London Magazine*.

Some of the poems appeared in the following pamphlets: *Five Poems* (Clutag Press), *Dialysis Days* (Grey Suit), *The Sorrow Club* (Clutag Press), *Tara Browne 1945–66* (Greville Press).

My thanks are due to the following friends: Colin Falck, Judith Palmer, Alan Jenkins, William Wootten, Neil Rennie and Hermine Demoriane.

The poem 'The Sorrow Club' was commissioned by Ruth Padel for a celebration of Miguel de Cervantes at King's College, London.

Contents

LINES OFF

The Conductor Raises His Arms

A crackle of expectation
a silence of suspense
as the needle touches down on the day,

everything standing up
straight and still
like iron filings magnetised,

the air blue-veined, faint-lined
with splashes of static
on gatepost and tile.

A sudden gust of electricity
slakes its thirst
among giant purple stems.

A dry pink light comes down
and a shadow orchestra
shimmers to life.

The conductor raises his arms
and taps the window sill.
A mist of strings

holds back the overture for a moment.
The grey drone of the lawn
hovers just above the ground.

The sun's brass section begins
with a fanfare of gold
as the main theme is introduced.

Bed of Nails

Days move diagonally across town,
meet other days
travelling in the opposite direction.
Let off the leash,
I was roaming the streets after dark,
looking for a thread
among neon petals
splashing in gutters,

when the screech of brakes
heralded my destruction.
How kind of someone, I thought,
to consider de-accelerating
on my behalf, no matter
that the gesture came too late
to save my life.
The moment of truth

took me by the scruff of the neck
and hurled me through
a plate glass window made of ice.
I shot down the face
of a glassy curve
and came to rest where I am,
in a crazy place, in a bloody experience.
Danger, fear, rage,

the onset of extreme emotion
resulted in a message
being flashed down my nervous system
to two tiny glands,
one on each kidney,
which went into high speed action
pumping a charge of fear
into my bloodstream. Late,

almost too late at night,
I found myself barely alive
on a bed of nails.
I burst from the wreckage
with a blinding shock
of hips and hair and shoulder blades,
streaming green light
because of something I thought.

Pepys Island

I went there myself as a young man,
on the South Atlantic voyage
of William Ambrose Cowley, privateer.
We had come into heavy seas
off Patagonia, when an uncharted island
rose above the waves,
offering us safe anchorage.
I saw its form of a shark's fin
cleaving the water, its strange alignment
of stunted trees dotting the horizon.
I remember, as if it were yesterday,
the jaws of a natural harbour
opening to receive us, yet nobody,
from that day to this,
has been able to find 'Pepys Island',
as we christened our discovery.
The only proof of its existence
lies in the pages of my log,
showing features of that blessed refuge
which I cling to as I write.
It saves me from shipwreck to this day.

Lines Off

I don't know whether to make
the difficult right-hand descent
by way of a crooked stair
with its missing steps
and multiple overhangs
and risk arriving late,
or take the vertiginous plunge
down the left-hand margin
and arrive ahead of myself.

I'd rather take the lift,
but where is it located
in this godforsaken building?
I can't make my entrance
suspended in mid-air, groping blindly
for non-existent bannisters.
I feel like turning back,
but it's too late for that now.
I'm going to have to jump.

Dear Arm

How many times, dear arm,
have you put yourself in danger
for my sake? How many times
have you found your way home
through the dark, or saved me from falling?
I didn't have to ask you twice.

Poor arm! I broke you once.
I burnt you once. More than once
I cursed your weakness
at arm-wrestling and swimming,
but I was proud of your tan
when I rolled up my sleeve at school.

You aren't so handsome now,
but you soldier on, one of the faithful
in my band of volunteers,
my noble standard bearer
in the war within a war,
the daily clash of purposes.

Dear arm, hold still for me now,
while I make you suffer once more.
Be brave, while the surgeon
creates an 'access fistula'
that will wash my blood for me.
It seems you must save my life as usual.

Dialysis Days

For the first time in my life
I have a regular job to go to.
Not a very good one perhaps,
but better than nothing
if you don't mind doing nothing for a living.
Unpaid of course, but the social worker
says she can get me £50 a week
'Attendance Allowance' if I'm lucky.
'They'll turn us down the first time we apply,
but we'll get it on appeal.'

She was right. All I have to do
is get myself to the workplace on time
and roll up a blood-stained sleeve.
I grab a sandwich at the Angel Pret,
then take the little 214 down Pentonville
to St Pancras Old Church Cemetery
with its workhouse out of *Oliver Twist*.
My job is holding out my hand
to a machine, palm up, like a beggar,
and doing my best not to move.

It's a leisurely life to be sure,
going somewhere, waiting there for four hours,
then going home again with a headache.
You wonder whether it's worth your while.
By half-time you're praying

for the squeal of the tea-trolley
coming round with its bonus
of lemon-flavoured crushed ice.
Now all you have to do is ask Yvette
to open your biscuits for you.

The Last of the Mohicans

Popeye greets the assembled corpses
in the Mary Rankin Dialysis Wing
with his usual 'Hi-de-hi, Campers.
The wanderer returns!
The Last of the Mohicans!'
I toss him his favourite 'Nice to see you'

and he doesn't let me down.
'Baby, it's cold outside' he shudders.
'A foggy day in London Town.'
He's Scott of the Antarctic,
The Spy Who Came in from the Cold,
Larry Grayson saying 'Shut that door!'

Or else he's mopping his brow
for 'It ain't half hot, Mum', sweating it out
in the Black Hole of Calcutta.
Polly puts the kettle on
and it's tea and biscuits for Les Misérables.
'Let them eat cake,' says Popeye.

Polly is up the Khyber again,
but there's no use crying over spilt milk.
'Tea for two and you for me,' sings Popeye.
'Buy one and get one free, eh?'
'The Battle of the Bulge?' I say.
'Great minds,' he tells me, winking happily.

My War

Not my mother,
but the mighty Nanny Henstock
was in charge of my defences in 1944.
She made me wrap up warm.
When invisible germans whined overhead
she wielded the big two-handed
Dettol-bottle sword
in case they were catching.
She was always blowing my nose.

Not my father,
but Flight-Sgt Stanley Ormond,
Nanny's Canadian boyfriend,
was our CO during the war.
He painted the camouflage
on replica Hurricanes and Mosquitoes
for the decoy aerodrome
at Dorney Reach.
He used the same paint
to camouflage my bedroom.

When my mother went up to London for the night
he would light his pipe
and put his feet up on the sofa.
He dragged my cot out of my bedroom
and on to the landing,
so that he and Nanny
could go to bed together.
They would slip some spearmint chewing gum
under my pillow
to keep my mouth shut.

Stanley used to knock out his pipe
in a hole in our apple tree,
making sparks fly.
The tree was my father,
puffing out sparks of pain.
I put my ear to the humming telephone poles
and heard his cries in Africa.
I didn't know who he was,
but my mother said
he was coming home on a leaf.

The Savoy Hotel in Wartime

'Good, good, excellent, splendid . . .'
said the maître d' of the Savoy Grill,
where dinner had recently ended.
'Good, good, excellent, splendid.'
They told him, 'To be perfectly candid,
it was enough to make anyone ill.'
'Good, good, excellent, splendid,'
said the maître d' of the Savoy Grill.

Teatime 1945

The sugar sandwich went out of focus
on its way to my mouth
when my soldier father
walked through the door in 1945.
I didn't catch his name,
but he seemed to know mine.

His smile filled the room
with an ominous cheerfulness.
He threw back his head
as if he owned the place.
What was he laughing about?
I couldn't understand his moustache.

His officer's uniform and hair
outranked my pale blue
siren-suit and matinée jacket.
His parting stood
like a feather in his cap,
as he advanced on my domain.

By the time we had finished tea
he had won the war. All that remained
was the transfer of my things
from my mother's bedroom
into the night nursery,
so I could wet the bed.

Fort Winter

None of us here at Fort Winter
will ever forget Suet Dumpling.
He was a regular comedian
with his cap perched on the side of his head
and his cheeky expression.
He made his classmates roar
with his Popeye routine,
or the axe buried in his skull.
His last words to his father
were that he'd scored a goal,
to his mother that he'd said his prayers.
He didn't want you to worry.

We washed and dressed him
in his regular blazer and shorts,
polished his shoes for him
and put a parting in his hair.
We laid him out for collection
by the window in Great Hall,
where the boys like to wait for their cars
on going-out days.
He'll be waiting for you there
when you come down next Sunday.
I think you'll agree that he looks
every inch the little gentleman.

True Detective

It was an old book about crime detection
with pictures of murders
and the places where they were committed,
including street plans
and details of how to get there.

You were supposed to solve the murders
then fill in the answers
in boxes. As you turned the pages
you rose through the ranks
to Detective Inspector.

If you failed to live up to
the challenge of a particular case,
or were outwitted by a suspect,
you found yourself back on the beat
as a police constable.

I struggled with my deductions,
but I kept losing my place
in the narrative, or being side-tracked
into following up false clues
and obvious red herrings.

Here was someone responsible
for breaking the news of a murder
to the victim's family,
who turned out to be the murderer himself.
I suppose I should have guessed.

Touch

My body is turning itself
into a makeshift kidney.
Pinheads of toxic waste
pop up like bad children
crying out for attention.

They run around all day
in their search for recognition.
One touch of a fingernail
and the little darlings sing
with short-lived satisfaction.

Shadow Pack

Business as usual?
The same again, landlord?
The mixture as before?
Or is everything different
now that everything exists
in a shadow pack?
I think about Portugal sometimes,
as if it were still there.

Either I draw the curtains
shutting out the light,
or I draw the curtains
letting in the night.
When the moon lays
two sheets of writing paper
on my bedroom floor,
I dwindle south in a sort of boat.

I'll never forget
the eager doing of nothing,
rolling it into balls
and placing them on shelves
the way we used to at the office.
I don't go there any more,
for I have gained
a poor understanding of time.

It darts about the place
in a pattern of lightning flashes:
a piebald, then a skewbald face,

expressing horror.
From a certain angle
it looks like a pantomime horse.
I turn it inside out
in case there is happiness in it.

I don't feel so confident
when a little broken shadow
creeps into my room.
I wonder what's the matter
with 60 watt bulbs these days.
They don't seem to light up
the way they used to.
I put it down to faulty wiring.

An Attendant Lord

Consider the post-war kids
growing up lonely and cool
in their bathroom mirrors.
Their hair is their poetry.
Their comb is their best friend.
They write their name with it.
They know there is someone waiting
in the wings of their life
and they think perhaps it is them.
Every slicked-back dreamer
turning up his collar
in the days before Teen
was auditioning the part of himself,
but only one man could win.

The rockabilly files at Sun
have plenty to say about the King,
but nothing at all about Jimmy Wages,
save that he existed
and sang 'Miss Pearl'.
'A shot in the dark might be
that he was related by marriage
to singer Mildred Wages
of Miller Sisters fame.'
He was an attendant lord
at the court of rock 'n' roll,
but whatever shades of obscurity
the world reserved for him,
it can't take away 'Miss Pearl'.

The Coming Out Ball

We took a ride on the Whip, on the Pirate Ship,
on the Helter Skelter, the Golden Galloper.
We climbed to the top of the Crater,
crashing down through the water,
on a Fordson tractor, on a Jensen Interceptor.
We were upside down in the Crazy Room,
rising and falling on the Haunted Swing.
We were holding our breath on the Wall of Death,
giving no thought to our means of transport
on the landslide down the mountainside,
on a Routemaster, on a combine harvester.
We were drinking and driving, barely surviving,
being carried about on a whale's spout,
through a bottleneck swirl, past the hat-check girl,
into the banqueting hall, the coming out ball.

A Pretty One

Whenever a tale is told
it becomes night,
then a young man in a white shirt
stands in the door of his house
and glances at his watch.
The young man in a white shirt
has all the time in the world
to light a last cigarette.
He's feeling confident tonight
as he contemplates his next move.

We can tell from the way
he steps down into the street,
expectant yet relaxed,
that his car is waiting nearby,
and later, hidden from us still,
a girl, a pretty one.
Whenever a tale is told
clouds pass across the moon.
A young man in a white shirt
holds out his hand for rain.

Tara Browne

(1945–1966)

I read the news today, oh boy,
about a lucky man who made the grade.
            – THE BEATLES, 'A Day in the Life'

If you'd apologised just once
for green shirts and amethyst cufflinks
you might have survived,
but who would have believed
that Irish-ironical 'Sorrry, sorrry'
as you fell about laughing?
You were only fifteen
when we followed you across Paris
after midnight, trying to keep up.
If our money ran out
you pretended to find a dix mille note
lying in the gutter – our student grant
for the further study
of Bloody Marys and rock 'n' roll.
You had the latest American singles
under your coat
in case the clubs weren't cool.

'Cut Across Shorty' by Eddie Cochran
was your signature tune
when you rubber-legged it across the floor
of the Club de l'Etoile,
smoking a Salem. After hours,
we took your portable singles player
to the Aérogare des Invalides,
its photomat and coffee machine,
dancing for the cleaners:

'Summertime Blues', 'C'mon Everybody'.
Our faces of children
are squashed together fighting
in the faded photo-strips.
We were still dancing
when Eddie flew through the windscreen
of a British taxi, followed to heaven
by his precious flame-coloured Gretsch.

We all came home from the party
safe and sound, but you didn't come home.
You went on into the night,
dancing your crazy doodle-step
on the pedals of your turquoise Lotus Elan,
till the music stopped
in the middle of Redcliffe Gardens,
at midnight, December 17th 1966.
It was the midway point
of a broken-backed decade.
Before it, the mini-skirt, the twist,
'I wanna hold your hand'. After it,
long hair, old clothes, 'A Day in the Life'.
Tara, the day you died
your friends went out of date.
Now there's a thought
you would definitely have agreed with.

Amtrak

Americans have left their things out to rust
beside the River Hudson. Cars and cranes and sheds
lie buried in foam at Roxy's Lighthouse.
LIQUID FLO-SWEET – SUGAR FOR INDUSTRY –
rolls backwards down THE ROUTE OF THE VISTA DOME.

In Albany, two wooden Indians stand guard
on top of Humpty's Hep Ur Sef. 'This here
is the Mohawk Valley we're entering . . .'
Old railroad workers, covered in fine white dust,
stare after us, licking chapped red lips.

Night Shift

Well, shepherd, well,
the golden age is gone
and I sit mumbling here.
My books keep watch on me.
I read them, feeling sorry for myself,
while all the time
a cyclorama of wind and stars
is being drawn across my sight.

Death has modified the house
for senior use, but gaps appear
when my body falls back on the bed.
O little room in my heart
with its view of paradise,
become my will
which won't agree with me.
Say no to me this once and I'll be good.

Surely it can be done
by stepping down into the street
and welcoming bad weather?
Are there not pleasures still to be had
in the smell of rain
on summer pavements, when night
trickles through a broken bottleneck?
I cup my hands like this.

A silent transaction
in the light of an open door.
What is being handed over?
What is being paid for?

The questions are hooks in a butcher's shop:
the black grease of fear,
flaming oil and such.
I make a mask out of fine gauze.

Day coming up on a dimmer switch,
taking over from the night shift.
A woodpecker's laugh
finds me tucked up in my cosy confessional.
I lie here forgiving myself
for the habit of mourning,
while all the time I am being carried
on great winds across the sky.

Party Casuals

Studio extras, party casuals like myself,
are equipped with little more
than a driving licence and cigarette lighter
for our life in films,
but we know how to stand around and talk,
so there's always work for us.

Jules Bar regulars, 400 Club faithfuls,
we drive down to Pinewood for the day
to collect our attendance fee
and pick up actresses. We depend on
plenty of re-calls and re-takes,
with a bonus for having our own top hat.

A friend is up for the ballroom scene
in *My Fair Lady*, lucky sod.
When I'm getting into my tails once more
to dance for my dinner in something like
Salad Days or *The Reluctant Deb*,
I can't help imagining

all those white ties and waistcoats
being washed and starched in lonely villages
by girls with red raw hands,
slaving over ironing boards and kitchen sinks.
I wonder if anyone
will ever make a film about one of them.

Ghost Signs

I was trying to read your mind
in London's palm, looking for reasons
in the windows of shops, the idiot
wisdom of traffic lights.
A ghost sign for REFRESHMENTS
high on a wall in York Way
and one for WEIGHING MACHINES
round the corner in Gray's Inn Road,
were growing fainter, harder to read.
The sun was going down
on the Poor School of Performing Arts,
Espiritu Santo Hairstyles and Nails,
'Hurricane Pool Hall Opening Soon'.
A battered tin advertisement
was spinning illegibly in the wind.

A Sailing Wind

We lie in bed all morning,
as if your going ended here
in this tender tangle
of bedclothes and breadcrumbs,
the last day of a month
gone on ahead of us.

For a month we have been
dying sulkily, our bodies
falsified, abandoned,
become symbols of treachery,
while you packed excitedly,
making ready to go.

This morning, curtains
blow through the open window.
The air is fresh.
The black damp has gone out of
the sunshine. We tear apart
and feel such ecstasy.

Big White Day

This must be the bad hairdresser,
the sculptress in lacquer
who backcombed your hair
into a prophetic helter-skelter.
She wanted to be paid in cash,
but £10 was a lot of money in 1968
and we only had traveller's cheques.
She accompanied us to the bank,
which made us late for the rehearsal.
The group gave us some Quaaludes
'to get you through your big day'
and we fell asleep in their minivan.
The last thing I remember
is Sam shouting 'Look out everyone,
my brother's been sick.'
The rest of the day's a blank.
Here's another one worth keeping,
taken with the flowers afterwards.
You're wearing the ring,
so we must have gone through with it.

Birdwatch

My window is a book of birds,
its fluttering pages
full of the usual conspirators
burying their secrets
in the background undergrowth,

when a freak of weather,
a sudden shaft of summer,
lightens the air around them
and there they all are,
scribbling their lives in the trees.

* * *

Today seems to be about magpies,
how they amuse themselves
hurling insults at everyone
and laughing at their own jokes.
They take a delight
in changing places with one another
for no particular reason,
till an old crow interrupts their game,
swearing loudly at them
and getting in the way.

I'm told magpies sulk
when they're upset, but not today.
They think it's hilarious
bouncing up and down on the catalpa tree,
making the beans jiggle and dance.

I'm starting to feel the same way
about my own life,
when a mindless streak of wood pigeon
crosses out the dream
with a single stroke of the pen.

* * *

Blues and greats compete for precedence
on their executive toy.
They're supposed to fly into the tree,
perch there for a moment, singing,
then find their way out
without touching anything.
They queue on a nearby branch,
impatiently waiting their turn.
They can't get enough of it.

The blues are constantly setting out,
then turning around in mid-air
and returning to their perch
to ruffle their feathers.
The greats never falter.
They fly straight in, sing their song
and fly out again.
They don't dither about like the blues.
You can't help rooting for the greats.

* * *

A blackbird revolves on a twig,
repeatedly changing its mind
about what to do next.

When it is facing right it is male.
When it is facing left it is female.
Just now it resembles both.

This is how blackbirds mate,
spinning like a weathervane in a squall,
until each turns into the other.

For a second the wind blows both ways.
The blackbird is pinned in mid-air,
like a coat-of-arms on a wall.

It suffers a confusion of colours,
a misunderstanding of feathers,
a sudden exchange of terrors.

When the weather returns to normal
the male flies off to the right,
the female to the left.

* * *

Bird in the holly tree,
invisible mentor,
your cheerful philosophy
is a glittering chain of light
slung between us,
drawing me ever closer
to your lonely joy.

The silver thread of your song
guides me through the dark
as surely as the night

I first heard you,
improvising on a theme
of beauty and truth
in the holly tree out there.

Poem

A random thought
or knock on the door
breaks through the carefully wrought
argument I'm working on
the way a twig or stem
breaks through the cigarette paper
I'm giving that final
twiddle and lick.

I'm about to give it that
final twiddle and lick
when a twig or stem
breaks through the carefully wrought
cigarette paper I'm working on
the way a random thought
or knock on the door
breaks through an argument.

Two Poets

I don't care about my great-grandfather,
'Hugh Williams of the Hundred Bastards',
Welsh patriot and political agitator,
lawyer brother-in-law of Richard Cobden.
He may or may not have taken part
in the Rebecca Riots of 1843, married late
into property, before settling down
to write battle hymns for Wales in English,
which he sent to Queen Victoria.

I prefer his son, my grandfather, also Hugh,
a consumptive poet and 90s dandy
who barely touched the surface of this world
before dying of spinal TB aged thirty-four.
He left behind a few poems in a drawer
and an unposted letter to his tailor,
describing, among other requirements,
the construction and location of a secret pocket
in the new suit he was planning.

His War

i.m. my grandfather-in-law Armand Dupuis 1891–1993

These are his things, his sword, his flag,
his hobby-horse, his globe,
all left behind in the nineteenth century,
put away for the Great War.
Here is his little pistolet,
his brass artillery cone,
his birthday card from Maman.
His soldiers wait in their box
for his return, still wearing
their blue and red Grande Armée uniforms.

Here is the map of Picardy
where he marked his house with a cross.
Here is the battlefield
where he rode to hounds as a boy.
He would spin the globe
and follow where it led,
but he had to turn back
when the war came to his gate.
Here is the mounting block
where he stood in his stirrups to salute.

At Verdun his thankless task
was stringing field telephones
between trenches. 'We were happy
when the helmets arrived from HQ.
Too late for some of us, alas.'
When his mother died
he asked his commanding officer

for leave to go to her funeral
and was given eight days in lock-up
for insubordination.

Home was a lifetime away,
down the road, when he recognised
his father's arab mare Palmyre,
filthy and thin from the war,
dragging an infantry wagon through mud.
He ran to greet his childhood friend
and she nuzzled his neck for a moment.
He kissed her goodbye,
then watched her disappear forever
into the noise and smoke.

The Deal

If you feel like a change
you can swap your present condition
for a case of dizziness,
bed for breathlessness,
cramps for unconsciousness.
You can lower your blood pressure
in return for a sick headache,
bore yourself to death
watching wheels going round,
or die of blood poisoning.

When you've cut some sort of deal
with the laws of nature
and passed another day on your back,
you can totter out of there
in thrall to the velvet hour,
sensing around you
the promise of night-scented streets
and the recklessness of summer.
You wonder what you would give
in exchange for this.

In My Absence

Dialysis two days running
produces an 'absence seizure',
a cerebral avalanche
of flints and sparks
which leaves me speechless.
I'm buried alive
in an abstract expression
of blizzards and ghosts,
blubbing, terrified, lost,
as I try but fail to exist.
The search for my face
in the snows of Mount Everest
is a hunt for the yeti
in the world of ideas.

The sort of thing I don't know
when I sit up in bed
and look in the palm of my hand
is why things happen when we do them
and not before.
It's funny at first
when you raise your hand
to touch the alien fur
and all of a sudden
you don't know who you are.
It's supposed to come back to you
like the name of the yeti,
but sometimes it doesn't
and they have to keep you in.

I've been trying to remember
the name of the beast
that has to forget itself
before it can begin.
I think it resembles
that of Alexander's horse,
the one named after a bull
because of his swollen head.
I want it tattooed on my arm
in case I'm washed up somewhere
without my medical notes.
Thank God for the lever beside my bed
which raises and lowers
the steeple of Highgate Church.

Consultation

If all else fails
we might try you on
Broncotriptolene,
the all-purpose
anti-viral blockbuster
known in the trade
as Tyrannosaurus Rex.

This predatory beast
undertakes a form
of ethnic cleansing
on your behalf,
tracking down
and exterminating
anything that moves.

Don't be alarmed.
According to its
manufacturer's warning
Broncotriptolene
impacts negatively
on your brain function
hardly at all.

X-Ray

They hold it up to the light,
incline their heads in consternation.

There it is as they had feared,
her name written across his heart.

Leaking Doctor

The doctor takes another sip
from his leaking coffee cup
and sets it down on my assessment form.

How am I feeling today?
Do my legs swell up at all?
Am I still working?

I move my arm up and down
and say I seem to be.
The doctor smiles and looks serious.

There is something we have to discuss
before he lets me go.
Do I have any brothers and sisters at all?

Coffee rings chase one another
round my assessment form.
The moment has come

when we have to talk about my case
'from the point of view of a transplant',
but I'm not to worry unduly.

Everything is going according to plan,
although he can't say where exactly.
He'll let me know.

Transplant 2014

I thought of the Old Operating Theatre
off Borough High Street,
'a marvel of the age' in 1821,
where students and doctors enjoyed
a state-of-the-art technology.
You enter via the spiral staircase
of the Southwark Cathedral Chapterhouse
and the antique smell of a herb loft,
looking down from the gods
on a wooden 'O', where the ghosts
of doctors and patients
rehearse their mortal pantomime.

The operating table takes centre stage
with its headrest and manacles,
its mop standing in a bucket,
its blood-stained aprons
hanging on a hook behind the door.
The vertiginous tiers of seating
have rails for the students to lean over,
drinking and shouting
to drown the screams of the principal,
as he struggles to free himself
from the terrible demands of his part.
He is giving the performance of a lifetime.

Fall Zone

(Royal Free Hospital)

Light piles up like snow
round the edges of table and chair,
suggesting the outline
of a mountain village,
a scarf of perfectly clear mist
suspended like a hammock
between two peaks.
I lie here, swaying to and fro.

I've lost the ability
to lift my sleeping head
out of the dreams and drifts
of avalanche weather,
but I have to make a start
on my study of the fall zone,
before I lose my way
in the storm of bedclothes overhead.

Lacking experience of the terrain,
I'm hiding in heaven
with my precious notebooks,
speaking in tongues
and eating my own prayers
for the amusement of the angels.
They laugh out loud
at my fearful prophecies.

I had travelled barely an inch
across the valley floor, on foot,
before turning around
and going home again, lost,
in a blizzard of crossings-out
and incorrections,
having failed to complete
my account of potential landslides.

I abandoned my plan
to produce a high-touring guide
for genuine mountaineers,
in favour of a warning alert
to casual visitors
not to venture at night
into the dreams and desires
of sleeping villagers.

Distant Grounds

Sitting here idly overlooking the sea,
watching the fishing boats setting out
for distant grounds,

seeing only her face, her arms, her neck,
the leisurely flow of her hips
rising and falling on the swell.

Skyros

The hard-pressed mother bird
takes the lift up and down
from her nest in the town
to the refuse-crowded beach.

Out of touch, out of reach,
the free-wheeling male
performs figure-eights
on up-draughts of warm air.

Homesick

The little scars on their faces
are the names of their villages,
put there when they were young
in case they got lost.

Their faces are maps
which they carry with them
when they set out across the world
for their new lives.

The scars look like the tracks of tears
cried for their childhood
as they move about their work
in our northern hospitals.

When they wake me in the night
to give me my medication
they shout my name
and shine a light in my eyes.

I wake, not knowing where I am.
The nurses and I are homesick,
crying to be taken home
to our lost villages.

Carphology

The delirious plucking at bedclothes
is all that remains
of a need we used to have
to do something useful with our lives.
Since we are here, we reason,
we might as well get on
with collecting bits of fluff
from our hospital blankets
and placing them in piles
against a rainy day.

For this is what we do now
and who we are – smoothers of surfaces
for dubious projects,
sweepers of refuse into
hopeless palaces,
rag-and-bone men of ourselves,
connoisseurs of ruin.
When a doctor diagnoses
'early onset carphology' he means
we haven't started eating our pyjamas yet.

TV Times

The gradual disappearance of one
familiar face after another,
to Manchester, or Ibiza,
or the ominous-sounding 'New Zealand',
fills the screen with ghosts,
who seem to exist in happier times.

The reason for their absence,
on holiday, or honeymoon, or merely
'steering clear of the Filth'
in Southend or the Algarve,
seems fair enough at the time
and the story carries on without them.

But when, after long months
of nobody mentioning their name,
they have failed to return to their duties
or contact their families,
we begin to suspect
that we may never see them again.

Over the years, their angry little world
has replaced itself many times,
while only a few stock characters
have stuck it out like the rest of us,
no longer available
for the more exciting plot-lines.

We have learnt to live with the fact
that anyone is liable to disappear,
then turn up later looking older and tired
in the hospital drama next door,
with some incurable disease
and no memory of their former lives.

The Leaving Test

Medical student Ari-Non
wants to see me taking a shower
to assess my hygiene skills
before he lets me go home.
His mouth turns down
when I express doubts about this,
but he says it doesn't matter
so long as I pass the shopping test.

He takes me downstairs in a wheelchair
and gets me to buy a newspaper
in the hospital shop.
I hesitate too long
between *The Mail* and *The Express*,
settling finally for *The Sun*.
Ari-Non looks dubious about this,
but he lets me carry on.

He tells me to check my change,
but it slips through my fingers
and runs around on the floor,
causing me to hallucinate briefly.
I make the mistake
of mentioning this to Ari-Non.
His mouth turns down
as he writes something in his book.

Going-Home Time

Pigeons on the starting-block
of the Time Flies clock
at going-home time
in Kensington Gardens.
We meet at Lost Children
near the defunct
Cow-Jumped-Over-The-Moon
water feature and drinking fountain.
Little broken men
climb the Elfin Oak
in their wire confinement.

No entrance permitted
to adults without children
to the Princess Diana Pirate Ship
(disarmed by popular demand).
Now jackdaws duel,
swallows are bows and arrows.
An afternoon with starlings
slides down the roof
of Never-Never-Land Entertainments.
A yellowhammer holds out
'a-little-bit-of-bread-and-no-cheese'.

Couple on a Bus

One minute gazing intently
into one another's eyes, the next

staring dully out of the window,
no longer beautiful, or young.

A New Country

Do you drop things? Do you trip
and hurl cups of tea ahead of you,
going upstairs? Do your possessions
have a life of their own
in which they dither idiotically
on your fingertips, then make a sudden leap?

In a flash they find their new home
in a dark corner of your room,
a distant country.
Your face turns red
and your head swells up like a balloon
as you make yourself bow down.

You see your own hand,
like someone else's hand,
two quivering fingers stretched out
to retrieve some random coin or pen,
before dropping it again
and kicking it further out of reach.

Do you have a grabber yet?
Or do you leave things where they are
in a tideline of debris
which crunches underfoot?
Do you shuffle along like that
in order to grind it into the carpet?

It seems to come naturally to you,
demonstrating your new talent
for imitating Harpo Marx –

joke hair on top, collapsible legs,
that hilarious expression of dismay
as you start to fall.

The Check-Up

'Oh yes, we thought he was a goner,'
the doctor tells his student nurse.
She looks at me admiringly,
imagining me dead. I take a little bow.
I always feel unwell when I hear the news
of my unscheduled return from the grave,
but I put on a brave face
and try to share their astonishment.
The doctor gets out his camera
and takes a picture of me alive.
The student poses smiling with the undead,
a willing witness to the miracle.
I put a friendly arm round her shoulders,
but spare her the vampire kiss.

The Love Field

Old people weren't born yesterday.
They remember the bombsite
on Shaftesbury Avenue.
They remember Danny Kaye.
They bought *It's Everly Time*
at Keith Prowse Records
opposite the Wimpy Bar.
They know which one is Phil.

Old people know where they are
most of the time
and they know where they used to be,
at the Café des Artistes in 1960.
When they try to go back
they aren't allowed in any more.
They can't help expressing
a low opinion of the place.

Some old men can still see and hear,
which makes you think
they may have other needs.
When they visit their girlfriends
late at night
they arrive out of breath,
in their Uni-Glo rough-sleeper,
their Sports Direct woolly hat.

Old people go out of their way
to appear knowledgeable
in the love field,
but the will is divided
against itself. The two-faced thing
exists in pain
and laughs at its own reasoning.
It makes itself cry.

In living we die apparently
and are snatched away
while we are still here,
replaced by something ignorant and poor:
another brow, another voice sounding.
Bad ideas dictate our future.
Foul-smelling draughts
accompany our progress through life.

The Sorrow Club

Once long ago at night
I was excited by rain
lighting the street for murder.
Was it too late, I wondered,
to do something stupid with my life?
Perhaps I was going to die myself one day?
Looking into the future
was like breaking open a thermometer.

I wanted to go out, of course,
in order to come home. But not too far.
A walk on the wild side
meant crossing the street occasionally,
to cheers from the neighbours.
Proceeding against my will,
I obstructed my own path,
I failed to look after myself.

My fault was wandering about
in a series of knight moves.
I was paying attention
to cherry blossom petals
trapped in the patterns of man-hole covers.
Faces without features
tore themselves to pieces before my eyes.
A reflection of my feelings, or their cause?

What was it that spoke to me like this
in the language of ribbons?
What trail of mischief fell from my hand
to bind me to itself?
I was looking for an ending
in the tangle of streets and thoughts,
when I noticed a quivering thing
tethered to a railing.

She told me to meet her at the Sorrow Club,
where a bad man greeted me
with sarcastic applause and blows.
I turned round fast and heard the click.
Little beads of mercury
were running around in the gutter.
Shadows fell from my blood. They carried me
shoulder-high through the night.

St Pancras Old Church and Hospital

I trace my footsteps
round this garden waiting room
where patients walk the line
between heaven and earth.

Great trees shed their prayers
on the silent company.
Stone books lie open forever
on forgotten endings.

I used to come here
every other day for years
with my books and sandwiches,
waiting to be reborn.

I would drag my feet
through the backsliding seasons
to a gate in the wall
with its notice of opening hours.

I passed my days
lying down with a machine,
till someone unknown to me died
and allowed me to go home.

Now here I am, a new man,
not quite myself perhaps,
yet able to ramble occasionally
in this twilit ante-room,
with only one foot in the grave.

The Half-Open Door

Walk along slowly
letting the rain come down
on head and shoulders,

or turn up my collar,
make a dash for it
and get wet all over?

Such were my thoughts
as I opened the front door
and almost went outside.

I feel like braving the weather
and making the most
of a free morning,

but the light has changed
and the air feels colder now
in the half-open door.

Hat or umbrella?
Raincoat or windbreaker?
It's hard to be sure

when the sun is shining
and rain is falling
from a clear blue sky.

Getting ready to go out,
time passes quickly.
Suddenly it's too late.